Macmillan/McGraw-Hill **TIMELINKS**

All Together

PROGRAM AUTHORS

James A. Banks
Kevin P. Colleary
Linda Greenow
Walter C. Parker
Emily M. Schell
Dinah Zike

CONTRIBUTORS

Raymond C. Jones
Irma M. Olmedo

Macmillan/McGraw-Hill

Citizenship

Students with print disabilities may be eligible to obtain an accessible, audio version of the pupil edition of this textbook. Please call Recording for the Blind & Dyslexic at 1-800-221-4792 for complete information.

learning through listening

The McGraw·Hill Companies

Macmillan McGraw-Hill

MHID 0-02-152399-1   ISBN 978-0-02-152399-3   Printed in the United States of America

2 3 4 5 6 7 8 9 10   058/043   13 12 11 10 09 08

All Together

Table of Contents

Unit 5 Our Government

VOTE

Vote

Skills and Features

Maps

Unit 5

EXPLORE The Big Idea

How do we get along together?

LOG ON

Find out more about how we get along together at www.macmillanmh.com

Our Government

People, Places, and Events

John Hancock

John Hancock was the first person to sign the Declaration of Independence.

LOG ON For more about People, Places, and Events, visit
www.macmillanmh.com

Philadelphia,
Pennsylvania

Philadelphia, Pennsylvania, is where the Declaration of Independence was signed.

American leaders **signed the Declaration of Independence** on July 4, 1776.

The Signing of the Declaration of Independence

Lesson 1

Vocabulary
holiday

Reading Skill
Main Idea and Details

Main Idea

Detail   Detail   Detail

A Call for Freedom

King George is not fair!

Freedom from King George

Working for freedom started long ago. The settlers from England felt that King George's rules were not fair.

On July 4, 1776, America's leaders wrote a paper. It said America was free from England. They called it the Declaration of Independence.

 Why did leaders write the Declaration of Independence?

John Hancock

A Free Country

John Hancock was the first leader to sign the Declaration of Independence. He wrote his name very large to make sure that King George could see it!

Event
July 4 Celebration

Every July 4, we celebrate our freedom. We wave flags. We have picnics and parades.

Americans celebrate the Declaration of Independence every July 4. It is a **holiday** called Independence Day. A holiday is a day to celebrate a famous person or event.

 How do we celebrate July 4?

Check Understanding

1. **Vocabulary** What is a **holiday**?

2. **Main Idea and Details** What happened on July 4, 1776?

3.  Why do Americans celebrate Independence Day?

A Plan for Our Country

Vocabulary
government

law

Reading Skill
Main Idea and Details

Main Idea

Detail Detail Detail

Our Government

Now that America was free from England, a new **government** was needed. A government is the group of people who run a country.

Our leaders had a meeting. They made a plan for a new government. They called this plan the Constitution.

 Why did our leaders meet?

Our Constitution

The Constitution is made up of rules for our country. The rules help us get along and keep us free.

Rules in government are called **laws**. Our Constitution has the most important laws in our country.

The Constitution says that we can choose our own leaders. It says that everyone is free to say or write what they think. The Constitution keeps things fair.

 What does our Constitution say?

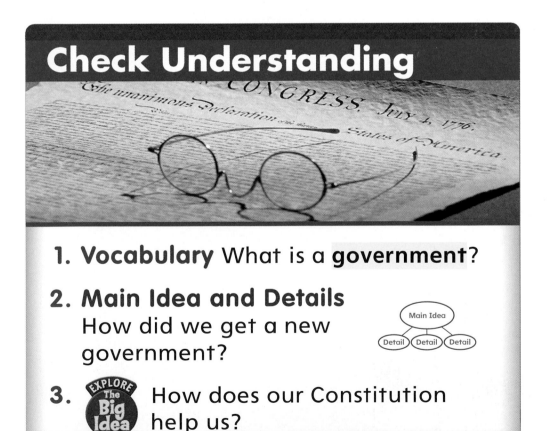

Check Understanding

1. **Vocabulary** What is a **government**?

2. **Main Idea and Details** How did we get a new government?

3. **EXPLORE The Big Idea** How does our Constitution help us?

All About Laws

Lesson 3

Reading Skill

Main Idea and Details

Main Idea

Detail   Detail   Detail

Laws for Our Country

Some laws are made for everyone in our country to follow. Other laws are made for our states and communities.

Everyone in the United States looks to see what the traffic light shows us. When we walk to a corner and the light is red, we stop!

 When do you stop at a corner?

Places
The Capitol Building in Washington, D.C.

The laws for our country are made in the Capitol Building. It is located in Washington, D.C.

State and Community Laws

In many states, like Michigan, we wear seat belts when we ride in a car. This law keeps us safe.

In Wichita, Kansas, it is the law to keep our sidewalks clear. This makes it safe for people to walk.

Sally has fun shoveling the snow in the winter. That way, people won't slip and fall!

 How does a clear sidewalk keep people safe?

Check Understanding

1. **Vocabulary** Why do we have **laws**?

2. **Main Idea and Details** Tell about a law in your community. How does it help people?

3. **EXPLORE The Big Idea** How do laws keep us safe?

Citizenship

Democracy in Action

Being Fair

We need to be fair to get along with each other. Read what Charles said when there were only two apples for four people.

Here are two apples.

But there are four of us.

Charles helped to make things fair.
What would you do?

I want my own apple!

We can cut them so we can all share.

What Can Citizens Do?

Lesson 4

Vocabulary

citizen

vote

picture graph

Reading Skill

Main Idea and Details

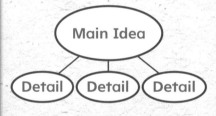

Good Citizens

The people who belong to our country are called **citizens**. Good citizens follow the laws of their country, state, and community.

Good citizens also help others. They work to make their neighborhoods and communities better and safer.

What is a citizen?

A Class Vote

Sometimes we do not all agree. A fair way to decide is to **vote**. A vote is a choice that can be counted.

Ms. Bell's class could not agree on a name for their class pet. Some wanted *Fluffy* and others wanted *Doodles*. Ms. Bell decided that a class vote was a fair way to choose the name.

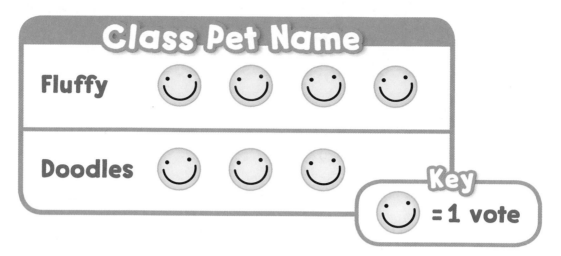

Class Pet Name

| Fluffy | 😊 😊 😊 😊 |
| Doodles | 😊 😊 😊 |

Key
😊 = 1 vote

This **picture graph** shows how Ms. Bell's class voted. A picture graph uses pictures to show the number of things. This one shows how many children voted for the names *Fluffy* and *Doodles*.

 Did more children vote for *Doodles* or for *Fluffy*?

Voting for Leaders

When a citizen is 18 years old, he or she can vote for new laws and government leaders. Voting is one more way to be a good citizen.

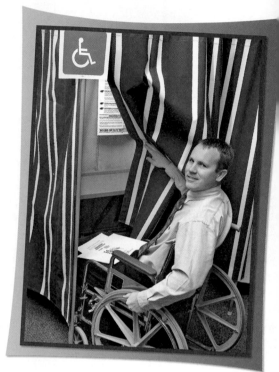

This man is going into a *voting booth*. A voting booth is a place to vote.

Around the World

Mauritius is an island country next to Africa. The people there vote for new laws and leaders. When Noor grows up, she will vote for laws and leaders, too.

Voting is important.
When a citizen votes he
or she helps to choose what
happens in our country.

 Why is voting a fair way to choose something?

Check Understanding

1. **Vocabulary** What does a good **citizen** do?

2. **Sequence** What can people do when they don't agree?

First
Next
Last

3. What makes a good citizen?

Our Leaders

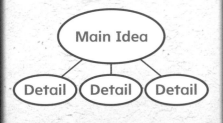

The President

Our President is the leader of our country. The President's job is to make sure that people in our country follow our country's laws.

The President lives in Washington, D.C. He lives and works in the White House.

 What does the President do?

White House

Oval Office

Governors

A **governor** is the leader of a state. The governor's job is to make sure that people follow that state's laws. The governor also works with others. He or she helps people in the state get services they need.

Jennifer Granholm is the governor of Michigan. She works in the Michigan State Capitol building. It is in the city of Lansing.

Many people in Michigan need jobs. Governor Granholm cares about them. She is working hard to get more jobs for the people of Michigan.

 What is a governor?

Community Leaders

The **mayor** is the leader of a community. He or she works in a building called city hall.

The mayor makes sure that people follow the laws of the community. He or she works with police to keep people safe.

People
Mayor Abdul Haidous

Abdul Haidous is the mayor of Wayne, Michigan. He is the first Arab American mayor in our country. He says, "I am grateful to live in the greatest nation on Earth."

The mayor cares about all of the people in a community. His or her job is to make life better for everyone.

 What is a mayor?

Check Understanding

1. **Vocabulary** What does a **governor** do?

2. **Sequence** What does the President do?

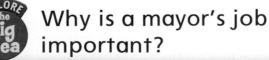

3. Why is a mayor's job important?

Use Directions

Vocabulary
directions

Directions tell us which way to go. North, south, east, and west are directions. These directions help us to find places.

North

Places to visit in Michigan

Lake Superior

MICHIGAN

Lake Huron

West

East

Map Key

Craig Lake State Park

Sturgeon Point Light House

Henry Ford Museum

Tulip Time Festival

Au Sable River

Lake Michigan

Lake Erie

South

Look at the map of Michigan on page 30. Touch the arrow that says south.

Now, move your finger up to the arrow that says north. In what direction are you moving?

Try the Skill

1. What are **directions**?

2. In what direction would you travel to get from the Henry Ford Museum to the Tulip Time Festival?

Writing Activity Write about a trip you have taken. Tell the directions.

The Statue of Liberty

We have special symbols that show we are proud of our country. The Statue of Liberty is a symbol of our country's freedom.

The Statue of Liberty was a gift to America from France. It was so big it had to be sent in hundreds of pieces!

 What statue is a symbol of our freedom?

Our Flag

A **flag** is a cloth with colors or pictures on it. We celebrate our country with the American flag.

Our flag is a symbol of our country. The colors on our flag are red, white, and blue. Our flag has 50 stars. There is a star for each one of our states.

We treat our flag with care. We wave our flag. We say the *Pledge of Allegiance* to it. To pledge allegiance means to promise to be loyal.

The Pledge of Allegiance

I pledge allegiance to the flag
of the United States of America
and to the Republic for which it stands,
one Nation under God, indivisible,
with liberty and justice for all.

 What do the stars on our flag stand for?

The Bald Eagle

The bald eagle is another symbol of our country. It is big and strong. Our country is big and strong, too.

bald eagle

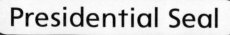

Presidential Seal

It is easy to find pictures of the bald eagle. It is on the seal that stands for our President. The bald eagle is on mailboxes and mail trucks. It is even on a quarter!

quarter

 What does the bald eagle stand for?

Comprehension Check

1. **Vocabulary** What is a **flag**?

2. **Main Idea and Details** What is on our country's flag?

3. What are some symbols that stand for our country?

Unit 5

Review and Assess

Vocabulary

Complete each sentence.

vote   **picture graph**   **directions**

1. We use _____ to tell us which way to go.

2. A choice that can be counted is called a _____ .

3. A _____ uses pictures to show the number of things.

Critical Thinking

4. How is voting a fair way to decide what to do?

5. Why is the Constitution important?

Map and Globe Skills

Look at the direction arrows on the map of Oklahoma.

6. In what direction would you travel to get from Black Mesa State Park to Tulsa Air and Space Museum?

A. north

B. south

C. east

The Big Idea — Government Activity

Vote for a Class Flag

1 Our country has a flag. Your class can have a flag, too.

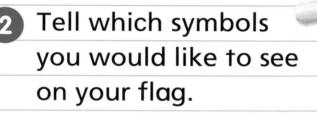

2 Tell which symbols you would like to see on your flag.

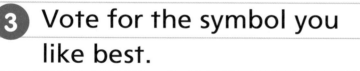

3 Vote for the symbol you like best.

4 Use the symbol to draw your class flag.

Grade 1 Stars

Picture Glossary

C

citizen A **citizen** is a person who belongs to a country. (page 19)

D

directions **Directions** tell us which way to go. (page 30)

F

flag A **flag** is a cloth with colors or pictures on it. (page 34)

G

government A **government** is the group of people who run a country. (page 9)

G

governor A **governor** is the leader of a state. (page 26)

H

holiday A **holiday** is a day to celebrate, or remember, a famous person or event. (page 7)

L

law A **law** is a rule in government. (page 10)

M

mayor A **mayor** is the leader of a community. (page 28)

P

picture graph A **picture graph** is a graph that uses pictures to show the number of things. (page 21)

V

vote A **vote** is a choice that can be counted. (page 20)

Index

This index lists many things you can find in your book. It tells the page numbers on which they are found. If you see the letter *m* before a page number, you will find a map on that page.

Index

Credits

Maps: XNR

Illustrations: 4: Judith Moffatt. 10-11: Judith Moffatt. 12: Christine Schneider. 14-15: Sharon Hawkins Vargo. 20-21: Maggie Smith.

Photography Credits: All Photographs are by Macmillan/McGraw-hill (MMH) except as noted below.

1: Jason Horowitz/zefa/CORBIS. 2: (l) The Granger Collection, New York; (r) Ingram Publishing/Alamy Images. 3: (b) Private Collection, Peter Newark American Pictures/Bridgeman Art Library; (t) CORBIS/PunchStock. 5: Bettmann/CORBIS. 6: (b) Ariel Skelley/Getty Images; (t) The Granger Collection, New York. 7: Bettmann/CORBIS. 8: Comstock/PunchStock. 9: age fotostock/SuperStock. 11: (c) Comstock/PunchStock. 13: SuperStock. 14: Randy Faris/CORBIS. 15: (c) SuperStock; (t) Rick Gomez/ Masterfile. 16: (bl) Ken Karp for MMH; (br) Ken Karp for MMH. 17: (bl) Ken Karp for MMH; (br) Ken Karp for MMH. 18: Dave Nagel/Getty Images. 19: Erik S. Lesser/AP Photos. 22: (b) Giraud Philippe/CORBIS SYGMA. 22: (t) Momentum Creative Group/Alamy Images. 24: Brooks Kraft/CORBIS. 25: (bl) Peter Gridley/Getty Images; (br) Wally McNamee/CORBIS. 26: Charlie Neibergall/AP Photos. 27: (bl) Al Goldis/AP Photos; (br) Gary Malerba/ AP Photos. 28: (br) Allen Brooks Photography; (l) Courtesy City of Wayne. 29: (b) Peter Gridley/Getty Images; (c) Courtesy City of Wayne; (t) Courtesy City of Wayne. 31: Carlos Osorio/AP Photos. 32: Bill Ross/CORBIS. 33: (bl) Bettmann/CORBIS; (br) Centennial Photographic Company/CORBIS. 34: CORBIS. 35: Digital Vision/ PunchStock. 36: (br) Bettmann/CORBIS. 36-37: (b) CORBIS. 37: (c) CORBIS; (t) Brand X Pictures/PunchStock. 38: Ingram Publishing/Alamy Images. 40: (t) Stephen Ogilvy for MMH. R1: (b) Charlie Neibergall/AP Photos; (bc) Pablo Martinez Monsivais, Pool/AP Photos; (c) CORBIS. R2: (b) Momentum Creative Group/Alamy Images; (c) Allen Brooks Photography; (t) Ariel Skelley/ Getty Images; (tc) Randy Faris/CORBIS.